STICKER SPOT IT

DOGS

D1324286

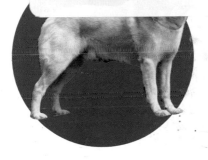

TOP THAT! Kids™

Copyright © 2004 Top That! Publishing plc
Tide Mill Way, Woodbridge, Suffolk, IP12 1AP, UK
www.topthatpublishing.com
Top That! Kids is a Trademark of Top That! Publishing plc

HOW TO USE YOUR SPOT IT GUIDE

Next time you dodge that bouncing bundle on a lead, why not take a closer look? Open your eyes wide to discover all about the dogs around you! There's 101 different types to spot.

Firstly, have fun attaching the specially-shaped stickers onto the outlines on some of the pages. There are matching numbers to help you.

SPOT IT! GOT IT!

When you've spotted something, stick in one of the round stickers, and make a note of when, and where, you saw it.

We've also rated the dogs according to how likely you are to see them. Ten points means you've spotted and scored an easy target while 60 points means you've found a really rare type! How long will it take you to reach the maximum score of 3,210?

HINTS AND TIPS
- Why not visit a dog show? It's a sure-fire way to spot those rarer breeds.
- Get out early to spot those dog walkers.
- Remember – whether you see the dog for real, on the Internet, in books, or magazines – they all count as 'Spots'!

WORKING DOGS

NAME: Anatolian Shepherd Dog **CLASS:** Working

I'm a big guy who originated in Turkey over 3,000 years ago. My strength and independence made me ideal for defending shepherds against dangerous predators. That's why I'll make a fantastic guard dog and loyal companion if I'm trained correctly. Look out for my short, colourful, patterned coat.

POINTS VALUE: 60

DATE SPOTTED:	SPOT IT!	GOT IT!
WHERE SPOTTED:		

- -

NAME: Bearded Collie **CLASS:** Working

Although I look really cute and slightly dopey, don't be fooled. Historically, my main job was to round up the herd and you may find it hard to control me when out in the field! My bad habits (which include barking a lot) may be hard to break, but I'm gentle with children. My thick coat needs lots of grooming. **POINTS VALUE:** 20

DATE SPOTTED:	SPOT IT!	GOT IT!
WHERE SPOTTED:		

NAME: Bernese Mountain Dog | **CLASS:** Working

I've got Swiss origins as you can probably tell from my name and come from the high hills of the Bern mountains. I'm strong, active, and make a good family pet. My strong, straight muzzle makes me very pretty to look at, and my coat is often 'tricoloured' (three colours). **POINTS VALUE:** 30

DATE SPOTTED: | **SPOT IT!** | **GOT IT!**
WHERE SPOTTED:

- -

NAME: Boxer

CLASS: Working

I'm a really popular breed as I'm totally devoted to my owners and will wait patiently, for hours, for their return. I'm not too keen on strangers, but I'm brave and will try anything once! My smooth coat reveals that I've got well-developed muscles that allow me to run about for hours. My tail is usually cut short.

POINTS VALUE: 20

DATE SPOTTED: | **SPOT IT!** | **GOT IT!**
WHERE SPOTTED:

NAME: Bullmastiff **CLASS:** Working

I've got a well-arched, muscular neck and a wide, deep chest which makes me very powerfully built. From my name you can tell that my parents were an English mastiff and a bulldog. I look pretty ferocious and, you bet, I  can be – I'm popular as a guard dog! Just as long as my owner is firm, I can be a loyal companion. **POINTS VALUE:** 30

DATE SPOTTED: **SPOT IT!** **GOT IT!**

WHERE SPOTTED:

NAME: German Shepherd **CLASS:** Working

A lot of people know me by another namo, tho Alsatian. I'm intelligent and I learn quickly, which means that I often work with the police force as a 'sniffer' dog. I'm also obedient and will act on instructions. Most of us are lean and fast, but we have a tendency to eat more than we should. **POINTS VALUE:** 10

DATE SPOTTED: **SPOT IT!** **GOT IT!**

WHERE SPOTTED:

NAME: Dobermann   **CLASS:** Working

Watch me run! I've got a lovely smooth, trot-like gait and can cover distances quickly. The distinctive markings on my face and body are often red and stand out against my dark, glossy coat. I was first bred by a tax collector, Dr Louis Dobermann, in the nineteenth century. **POINTS VALUE:** 10

DATE SPOTTED: **SPOT IT!**   **GOT IT!**

WHERE SPOTTED:

. . . .

NAME: Great Dane   **CLASS:** Working

My sleek coat comes in many colours, from light cream to black. I'm probably a cross between a mastiff and a greyhound, which makes me strong and also very fast! As a hunting dog I'm second to none and, historically, would have dared to tackle a wild boar. If you give me lots of room and exercise, I'll make a friendly household pet.

POINTS VALUE: 20

DATE SPOTTED: **SPOT IT!**   **GOT IT!**

WHERE SPOTTED:

NAME: Giant Schnauzer

CLASS: Working

When standing upright, I form an angular shape. My face is nearly always dark and I am a particularly handsome dog when my coat is all black. My wiry top coat allows me to survive harsh weather conditions.

POINTS VALUE: 40

DATE SPOTTED: SPOT IT!   GOT IT!

WHERE SPOTTED:

NAME: Belgian Sheepdog   **CLASS:** Working

Sometimes known as the Groenandael, or Chien de Berger Belge, in WW1, I carried messages to the battlefields and even pulled machine guns.

POINTS VALUE: 50

DATE SPOTTED: SPOT IT!   GOT IT!

WHERE SPOTTED:

NAME: Old English Sheepdog

CLASS: Working

I made my acting debut when promoting a famous British brand of paint. I look adorable yet slightly dim – but my furry coat covers my quick, intelligent eyes and I'm great at guarding sheep. Some know me as the 'bobtail' because of my docked tail. **POINTS VALUE:** 20

DATE SPOTTED: SPOT IT!   GOT IT!

WHERE SPOTTED:

NAME: Pinscher **CLASS:** Working

I'm an old German breed with an elegant stature and beautifully smooth coat which is easy to look after. In fact, I make a good all-round house dog, as I'm of medium size and very clean! I'm also lively and love to play. I can make an ideal guard dog in the smaller home. **POINTS VALUE:** 30

DATE SPOTTED: **SPOT IT!** **GOT IT!**
WHERE SPOTTED:

- -

NAME: Rottweiler **CLASS:** Working

I'm pretty big and powerful! With my natural guarding instincts, I'm another favourite when it comes to protecting people and their property. I don't get nervous easily, and I'm compact and strong. However, don't believe the hype about my vicious personality – careful training and sensible ownership will bring out my willing side. **POINTS VALUE:** 10

DATE SPOTTED: **SPOT IT!** **GOT IT!**
WHERE SPOTTED:

8

NAME: St Bernard   **CLASS:** Working

I'm at home covering all types of terrain which makes me ideal for rescuing people in the mountains. I've got a slow, unhurried gait and always look where I'm going. My huge size means that I can weigh as much as a human adult

and will eat much more! If you've got loads of room to let me run around, and a large budget, then I'll make a wonderful companion.

POINTS VALUE: 30

DATE SPOTTED: **SPOT IT!**   **GOT IT!**

WHERE SPOTTED:

. . . .

NAME: Samoyed   **CLASS:** Working

Would you believe from my stunning looks that I was actually bred in remote regions of Russia, and can survive the toughest conditions and can herd other animals? I'm striking, graceful, very affectionate and will make a great pet for anyone who has the time to look after my thick coat! **POINTS VALUE:** 30

DATE SPOTTED: **SPOT IT!**   **GOT IT!**

WHERE SPOTTED:

9

NAME: Alaskan Malamute   **CLASS:** Working

I'm a large, incredibly hardy dog who is used to pulling sleds. Heavy loads are not a problem for me! This means that I require a lot of exercise and good feeding. Whilst some people keep me as a pet, I am not necessary loyal so do not make the best guard dog. **POINTS VALUE:** 40

DATE SPOTTED: **SPOT IT!**   **GOT IT!**

WHERE SPOTTED:

NAME: Australian Cattle Dog   **CLASS:** Working

I'm known as a 'heeler' because of the way I'll nip the heels of those who refuse to be herded! I'm very strong and brave and will guard my 'shepherd', his possessions and his land to the end. My mottled colouring is particularly distinctive. A true working dog, I do not make the best pet because I need to have lots to do.
POINTS VALUE: 60

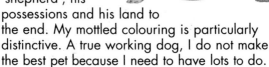

DATE SPOTTED: **SPOT IT!**   **GOT IT!**

WHERE SPOTTED:

NAME: Siberian Husky

CLASS: Working

Some people still think of me as a 'wolfish' creature, but I am 100 per cent dog! I was developed by the Chukchi people of Northeast Asia to pull sleds. Nowadays, a growing number of people wish to keep me as a pet. **POINTS VALUE:** 50

DATE SPOTTED: SPOT IT!   GOT IT!

WHERE SPOTTED:

NAME: Border Collie **CLASS:** Working

I like nothing more than being out in the field rounding up sheep, and am stealthy and fast. We're a very intelligent breed that thrives on work. Lots of exercise is vital to prevent boredom and anxiety setting in. **POINTS VALUE:** 10

DATE SPOTTED: SPOT IT!   GOT IT!

WHERE SPOTTED:

NAME: Saluki

CLASS: Working

With my thick, corded coat covering my eyes, I may look funny but I'd be lost without it when herding cattle and sheep in my native Hungary. The top coat defends against all weathers, and the softer, dense undercoat keeps me really warm. I'm a hardy dog who can make a great pet. **POINTS VALUE:** 50

DATE SPOTTED: SPOT IT!   GOT IT!

WHERE SPOTTED:

UTILITY DOGS

NAME: Boston Terrier **CLASS:** Utility

My short, stocky body makes me a bit of a heavyweight, and I've got a definite 'bull' look, with my squashed muzzle and well-built legs. When running, I'm quite fast and have a surprisingly perfect rhythm. Although I can be a bit naughty (I have a mind of my own!) – I'm still loads of fun and have bags of energy. **POINTS VALUE:** 30

DATE SPOTTED: **SPOT IT!**   **GOT IT!**

WHERE SPOTTED:

- -

NAME: Bulldog **CLASS:** Utility

Although I'm not the most attractive dog on the block, there are good reasons why I'm a British icon. I can be a little fierce, but very loyal to my family. I'm also affectionate and generally happy, despite my face which makes me look constantly annoyed! My widely spaced forelegs means that I'm also very strong. **POINTS VALUE:** 40

DATE SPOTTED: **SPOT IT!**   **GOT IT!**

WHERE SPOTTED:

NAME: Chow Chow **CLASS:** Utility

I'm like a lion (leonine) in appearance, with my large neck frill, thick coat and bushy tail. Other things that make me look even more unusual are my tongue and gums which are a blue/black colour. I'm a loyal companion, but treat strangers with aloofness. My close-set ears mean that I look like I'm scowling when I'm not!

POINTS VALUE: 40

DATE SPOTTED: **SPOT IT!**   **GOT IT!**

WHERE SPOTTED:

. . . .

NAME: Dalmatian **CLASS:** Utility

The more geographically-minded of you might think that I'm from Dalmatia (a part of Croatia), but the modern version of my breed was introduced to England in the nineteenth century. My first job was to follow the carriages of well-off types. Now, I make an affectionate, loyal pet, but my owner needs to have as much stamina as me!

POINTS VALUE: 20

DATE SPOTTED: **SPOT IT!**   **GOT IT!**

WHERE SPOTTED:

I'm a pretty strong all-rounder when it comes to being a good pet. I'm happy, alert and totally devoted to my family. If you want to go for a walk, I'll be right there at your heels and ready for action! My coat actually has two layers. The underneath is short and woolly, but my top coat is straight. **POINTS VALUE:** 30

DATE SPOTTED:　　　　　　**SPOT IT!**　**GOT IT!**

WHERE SPOTTED:

NAME: Japanese Spitz　　**CLASS:** Utility

I've become a real favourite in recent years. My pure white coat is eye-catching, and I'm alert and lively. To keep me looking good, I'll need a fair amount of washing and brushing, but I'll reward you by being a good household pet and watchdog. Strangers are always desperate to stroke my beautiful coat, but I can be a little shy of them. **POINTS VALUE:** 50

DATE SPOTTED:　　　　　　**SPOT IT!**　**GOT IT!**

WHERE SPOTTED:

NAME: Keeshond

CLASS: Utility

I'm often known as the Dutch Barge Dog, despite probably coming from Germany. You can take me out in rain or snow and my coat will still keep me warm and cosy. While I may look soft and cuddly, my coat is really coarse! **POINTS VALUE:** 20

DATE SPOTTED:	SPOT IT!	GOT IT!
WHERE SPOTTED:		

NAME: Miniature Schnauzer **CLASS:** Utility

My salt-and-pepper colouring makes me an interesting dog to look at, and my nearly 'square' shape ensures that I'm a hardy little fellow! I can run with real vigour and I'm also very brave. **POINTS VALUE:** 20

DATE SPOTTED:	SPOT IT!	GOT IT!
WHERE SPOTTED:		

NAME: Poodle **CLASS:** Utility

There are three types of poodle, standard, miniature and toy, and we were originally bred to fetch things out of the water. Take me down to a lake today and I'll still enjoy a splash about! Without a traditional 'lion' clip, I would be totally covered in fluffy hair. I'm an intelligent breed, and very clean. **POINTS VALUE:** 10

DATE SPOTTED:	SPOT IT!	GOT IT!
WHERE SPOTTED:		

NAME: Shar Pei   **CLASS:** Utility

As you can probably tell from my name I originated in China and, like other breeds from this country, I am quite independent. My coat is like a bristly carpet and we have folds in our skin (some being more wrinkly than others!) The skin over my eyes makes me look discontented but I'm very affectionate. **POINTS VALUE:** 60

DATE SPOTTED: SPOT IT!   GOT IT!

WHERE SPOTTED:

• •

NAME: Shih Tzu

CLASS: Utility

If you are willing to look after my long coat and indulge my fun-loving personality, then I'm a great pet for people with only a little room. My face is often compared to the chrysanthemum flower and is very appealing! It's really important that the hair over my eyes is tied out of the way – it's not just my owner wanting me to look pretty! **POINTS VALUE:** 30

DATE SPOTTED: SPOT IT!   GOT IT!

WHERE SPOTTED:

NAME: Tibetan Terrier | **CLASS:** Utility

I'm a good-looking dog whose long coat and smiling expression don't give away the fact that I was bred in Tibet to herd cattle. As such, I'm game for anything and will make you laugh with my sometimes madcap antics. My double coat means that I keep dry underneath whilst braving almost any type of weather.

POINTS VALUE: 50

DATE SPOTTED: | SPOT IT! | GOT IT!
WHERE SPOTTED:

- -

NAME: Canaan Dog | **CLASS:** Utility

With my dark, almond-shaped eyes I have quite a regal air. It's claimed that I'm the national dog of Israel and there is a touch of the semi-wild about me as my distant relatives are the pariah dogs of the Middle East. When I'm excited, my plumed tail curls over my back. I also respond well to training. **POINTS VALUE:** 60

DATE SPOTTED: | SPOT IT! | GOT IT!
WHERE SPOTTED:

NAME: French Bulldog **CLASS:** Utility

I certainly like my creature comforts so I make an ideal house pet. I'm the right size too, if you don't have much space. My most distinctive features are my short, undocked tail and my bat-like ears. I may look fierce, but I'm actually calm with a friendly personality. **POINTS VALUE:** 30

DATE SPOTTED: SPOT IT!   GOT IT!

WHERE SPOTTED:

NAME: Akita

CLASS: Utility

In the UK, I'm known by this name, but other countries differentiate between the Japanese and American variety. I'm a breed with ancient origins dating back approximately 4,000 years to the Japanese island of Honshu. I stand around an impressive 66 cm high and am well built with a docile nature. **POINTS VALUE:** 30

DATE SPOTTED: SPOT IT!   GOT IT!

WHERE SPOTTED:

NAME: Lhasa Apso

CLASS: Utility

My wise face seems suited to my origins as a mountain dog of Tibet. It was useful to have such a long, thick coat, as I faced freezing conditions. My ears are heavily feathered and mingle with my coat, which must be well combed. **POINTS VALUE:** 30

DATE SPOTTED: **SPOT IT!**   **GOT IT!**

WHERE SPOTTED:

· ·

NAME: Schipperke   **CLASS:** Utility

I'm a fairly cobby-looking (broad) dog with spitz blood. I originated from Flanders where my main purpose was to catch rats and other pesky vermin. As a pet, I make for a lively and amenable companion. **POINTS VALUE:** 30

DATE SPOTTED: **SPOT IT!**   **GOT IT!**

WHERE SPOTTED:

· ·

NAME: Leonberger   **CLASS:** Utility

If you're looking for a good guard dog with plenty of confidence, then I could be the one for you. I stand at an impressive height of around 75 cm and it comes as no surprise that I'm related to the Newfoundland, Saint Bernard and possibly, a mountain dog of the Pyrenees. **POINTS VALUE:** 60

DATE SPOTTED: **SPOT IT!**   **GOT IT!**

WHERE SPOTTED:

GUNDOGS

NAME: Brittany **CLASS:** Gundog

We Brittanys don't have 'standard' colouring as we vary a lot and commonly have three colours (tricolour). I'm a willing worker and a great retriever of game at shoots, but as you'd expect from a gundog, I need lots of exercise. I am responsive to training and have a 'happy' look! **POINTS VALUE:** 50

DATE SPOTTED: **SPOT IT!** **GOT IT!**

WHERE SPOTTED:

NAME: English Setter **CLASS:** Gundog

When I was first trained to retrieve dead or injured game, I'd crouch down to indicate where the bird was. Now, we setters tend to stand still, and even 'point' to the direction of the find with our muzzle. I'm very keen to find the scent when out and about, and make a handsome sight with my fine, silky coat with some feathering. **POINTS VALUE:** 20

DATE SPOTTED: **SPOT IT!** **GOT IT!**

WHERE SPOTTED:

NAME: German Short-Haired Pointer

CLASS: Gundog

My close relation, the Pointer, is similar in habits but rather larger. While he or she will 'point' to the game, I'll actually 'retrieve' it too! I've got a very keen nose and am good at tracking down the scent over both land and water. I've got a lovely short coat that requires a minimum of grooming (and doesn't shed all over the carpet). **POINTS VALUE:** 20

DATE SPOTTED:	SPOT IT!	GOT IT!
WHERE SPOTTED:		

· ·

NAME: Hungarian Vizsla **CLASS:** Gundog

With my russet-gold coat, I'm a real beauty and, despite my European origins, I'm beginning to be seen more and more around Britain. I'm good at both pointing and retrieving and I'm willing to please. My protective instinct means I've got a touch of the guard dog about me, and I'm good tempered around the family. **POINTS VALUE:** 60

DATE SPOTTED:	SPOT IT!	GOT I
WHERE SPOTTED:		

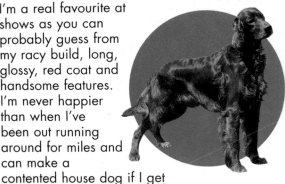

NAME: Irish Setter   **CLASS:** Gundog

I'm a real favourite at shows as you can probably guess from my racy build, long, glossy, red coat and handsome features. I'm never happier than when I've been out running around for miles and can make a contented house dog if I get enough exercise. **POINTS VALUE:** 10

DATE SPOTTED: **SPOT IT!**   **GOT IT!**
WHERE SPOTTED:

· ·

NAME: Pointer

CLASS: Gundog

I carry myself with real poise and make a handsome sight with my graceful curves. I'm fast and can work for long periods without getting tired. When I catch the scent, I'll point in the direction of the animal with my muscly neck.
I'm probably best suited to life in the country. My coat is usually white with lemon, liver or orange markings. **POINTS VALUE:** 20

DATE SPOTTED: **SPOT IT!**   **GOT IT!**
WHERE SPOTTED:

NAME: Golden Retriever

CLASS: Gundog

I'm a real star of the doggie world. As well as being a good retriever, I've been trained to 'sniff' out illegal substances and explosives, guide the blind and provide companionship for the elderly. I'm easy to train and am very cute. **POINTS VALUE:** 10

DATE SPOTTED: **SPOT IT!**   **GOT IT!**

WHERE SPOTTED:

. . . .

NAME: Labrador Retriever   **CLASS:** Retriever

I'm a broad, handsome dog that flourishes given enough exercise. Owners need to watch out for my large appetite, as I can easily overeat. I love to romp in the countryside, including in the water! **POINTS VALUE:** 10

DATE SPOTTED: **SPOT IT!**   **GOT IT!**

WHERE SPOTTED:

. . . .

NAME: Cocker Spaniel

CLASS: Gundog

I'm a sporting dog, and can cover good distances with my strong forelegs. I make a fun-loving household pet and children will adore my friendly nature and huge eyes. My coat is silky, and owners must be careful to keep my long, curled ears free of dirt. **POINTS VALUE:** 10

DATE SPOTTED: **SPOT IT!**   **GOT IT!**

WHERE SPOTTED:

(**NAME:** English Springer Spaniel) (**CLASS:** Gundog)

Springer by name, springer by nature! In gundog terms, 'to spring' means to flush game from their hiding places, but take me for a walk and I'll go several times the distance required to get from A to B, and still have some energy left! I was originally bred to find falcons as well as game. **POINTS VALUE:** 10

(DATE SPOTTED:) (SPOT IT!) (GOT IT!)
(WHERE SPOTTED:)

- -

(**NAME:** Weimaraner)
(**CLASS:** Gundog)

You'll either love or hate my appearance, but I certainly stand out from the crowd with my sleek, light grey coat, strong build and unusual light eyes. As a gundog, I can pretty much do it all, whether it's pointing or retrieving. Double-check what breed I am by looking out for an eel stripe down my back.
POINTS VALUE: 40

(DATE SPOTTED:) (SPOT IT!) (GOT IT!)
(WHERE SPOTTED:)

NAME: Italian Spinone | **CLASS:** Gundog

I'm happy whether I'm at home, or out for a day's shoot. I make an ideal companion for the hunt as I can adapt to almost all types of terrain, including water. I'm also patient and docile. I'm easy to spot as the majority of

us have a wiry, cream-coloured coat. I originate from France, but spent more time in Italy as our breed developed. **POINTS VALUE:** 60

DATE SPOTTED: | SPOT IT! | GOT IT!

WHERE SPOTTED:

• •

NAME: Chesapeake Bay Retriever

CLASS: Gundog

There's a bit of a story attached to my breeding. Most people think that I'm the result of a cross between either a Labrador or Newfoundland with the local breeds found in Chesapeake Bay, after a shipwreck near Maryland, USA in 1807. It is perhaps because of this that I have a great love of water. **POINTS VALUE:** 50

DATE SPOTTED: | SPOT IT! | GOT IT!

WHERE SPOTTED:

HOUNDS

NAME: Afghan Hound

CLASS: Hound

My Eastern-Oriental expression, along with my name, gives away the fact that I was bred in Afghanistan, where I'm still used for hunting and herding. I carry myself with great dignity and look impressive when my coat is brought into tip-top condition.

POINTS VALUE: 30

DATE SPOTTED:

WHERE SPOTTED:

SPOT IT!   **GOT IT!**

- -

NAME: Basenji

CLASS: Hound

You won't realise my stand-out feature just by looking at me – but you'll know when I make a noise as it is far more of a 'yodel' than a bark. I'm a pretty, elegant breed with a light build which resembles that of a gazelle. I make a good house dog for the loving-but-firm owner as I am clean and affectionate – but I sometimes have a mind of my own! **POINTS VALUE:** 40

DATE SPOTTED:

WHERE SPOTTED:

SPOT IT!   **GOT IT!**

NAME: Basset Hound

CLASS: Hound

I can tip the scales at 32 kg (70 lb) and can carry a lot of weight on my short legs. I'm a comical character with my lozenge-shaped body, massive feet and loose skin around my front. If I'm kept fit, I'm capable of impressive endurance. **POINTS VALUE:** 30

DATE SPOTTED: | **SPOT IT!** | **GOT IT!**
WHERE SPOTTED:

. . . .

NAME: Beagle | **CLASS:** Hound

I was bred to hunt hares, which meant I had to be very fast and capable of travelling fairly long distances across fields. I'm a sturdy, good-looking dog and make a great house pet as I'm fun and lively. **POINTS VALUE:** 30

DATE SPOTTED: | **SPOT IT!** | **GOT IT!**
WHERE SPOTTED:

. . . .

NAME: Borzoi

CLASS: Hound

I'm a tall, dignified-looking hound for the seriously enthusiastic owner only. Prior to the nineteenth century, my main purpose was to hunt hares and foxes, but given my size and stamina, breeders aimed to add enough bulk to my frame to hunt wolves. My long coat and neck frill require much attention! **POINTS VALUE:** 30

DATE SPOTTED: | **SPOT IT!** | **GOT IT!**
WHERE SPOTTED:

NAME: Bloodhound   **CLASS:** Hound

I'm named after my ability to pick up a scent, even hours after the trail has gone cold. I'm noble in carriage and not the kind of dog that scarpers about. I look pretty solemn and can be surprisingly shy. My short coat is really weatherproof which is great if I have to be out and about at all hours.

POINTS VALUE: 30

DATE SPOTTED: **SPOT IT!**   **GOT IT!**

WHERE SPOTTED:

· ·

NAME: Dachshund   **CLASS:** Hound

With my long body, I am ideally shaped to squeeze into a badger's sett to drive it out into the open. No surprise then, that my name in German means 'badger dog!'. I've got a strong bite which is essential when I have to confront such a fierce opponent. There are six varieties of my breed, including miniature and standard. **POINTS VALUE:** 10

DATE SPOTTED: **SPOT IT!**   **GOT IT!**

WHERE SPOTTED:

28

NAME: Finnish Spitz | **CLASS:** Hound

I'm a handsome dog with a plumed tail that can fold right over my back and a lion-like ruff around my neck. My coat is fairly rough and is easier to look after than it appears. I'm good at hunting birds and small game and I'm eager to get out into the field. We males are slightly larger and have more hair than our female counterparts. **POINTS VALUE:** 50

DATE SPOTTED: | SPOT IT! | GOT IT!

WHERE SPOTTED:

. . . .

NAME: Greyhound | **CLASS:** Hound

I'm a dog with a split personality! I've been bred to chase the fastest- running animals as soon as I've spotted them, and to kill them on the spot. Once I get home however, I'm a highly affectionate dog and very gentle. With my taut muscles and fine bone structure, I'm a great running machine with a supple gait.

POINTS VALUE: 10

DATE SPOTTED: | SPOT IT! | GOT IT!

WHERE SPOTTED:

NAME: Hamiltonstovare **CLASS:** Hound

In my homeland of Sweden I am used more as a lone hunter, although in other countries I often join a pack. I was named after the Swedish hunter, Hamilton, and am as hardy as they come. My 'tricolouring' is very distinctive and clearly defined.

POINTS VALUE: 60

DATE SPOTTED: SPOT IT!   GOT IT!

WHERE SPOTTED:

· ·

NAME: Irish Wolfhound

CLASS: Hound

I stand at least an impressive 79 cm (31 in.) high and you can see why I was originally bred to hunt such fearsome opponents as stags, bears and wolves. Unlike these beasts however, I'm a really gentle creature at heart. The wiry hair that hangs over my eyes and around my jaw is quite rough. My eyes are tranquil and belie my speed and courage.

POINTS VALUE: 30

DATE SPOTTED: SPOT IT!   GOT IT!

WHERE SPOTTED:

NAME: Petit Basset Griffon Vendeen

CLASS: Hound

I might be short but I can easily withstand a day's hunting on foot and have a strong nose for the trail. I've got a very appealing expression, and can be a favourite with children. **POINTS VALUE:** 50

| DATE SPOTTED: | SPOT IT! | GOT IT! |
| WHERE SPOTTED: | | |

NAME: Pharaoh Hound **CLASS:** Hound

I'm a unusual-looking dog with my fox-like head and amber eyes. We have only really been bred in Britain since being introduced from Malta in the 1970s.

POINTS VALUE: 60

| DATE SPOTTED: | SPOT IT! | GOT IT! |
| WHERE SPOTTED: | | |

NAME: Rhodesian Ridgeback

CLASS: Hound

Take a look at my back and you'll see that the hair grows in two different directions, forming two whorls on my shoulders. My colouring is most attractive and you'll find breeds ranging from a light red to dark chestnut. I like to play exciting games with the family and will protect them well. **POINTS VALUE:** 40

| DATE SPOTTED: | SPOT IT! | GOT IT! |
| WHERE SPOTTED: | | |

NAME: Saluki   **CLASS:** Hound

It is difficult to pinpoint my exact area of origin but it's safe to say that I have a strong element of the Middle East about me. There, my speed and hunting abilities were used to chase hares, jackals, and even gazelles. My grace, strength and beauty make me an appealing choice for a pet, but I need to be kept busy. **POINTS VALUE:** 30

DATE SPOTTED: **SPOT IT!**   **GOT IT!**

WHERE SPOTTED:

· ·

NAME: Whippet   **CLASS:** Hound

I'm easily identified by my muscular, lean body and deep girth. Despite looking similar to the greyhound, I am about 20 cm (8 in.) smaller in height. I could be described as the 'poacher's friend' due to my great rabbit-catching ability. My short coat means that I make a clean pet, and I'm loving and affectionate. Just remember that I thrive on lots of exercise!

POINTS VALUE: 10

DATE SPOTTED: **SPOT IT!**   **GOT IT!**

WHERE SPOTTED:

NAME: Deerhound **CLASS:** Hound

I'm a dog of great reputation, probably because I have the speed and strength to bring down a stag, but still carry myself with great dignity. My rough coat gives me the appearance of a greyhound with rough hair! I was developed in Scotland and have a long history. I'm eager to please and will be a good pet – but I stand at over 70 cm (28 in.) high!

POINTS VALUE: 60

DATE SPOTTED: **SPOT IT!**   **GOT IT!**

WHERE SPOTTED:

· ·

NAME: Elkhound **CLASS:** Hound

An elk is a large deer and I was bred to hunt them in my native home of Norway. I'm a hardy dog so I'm able to withstand freezing temperatures. Among my distinctive features is my tightly-curled tail. I need to be kept on a strict diet to stop me becoming overweight as I'm of a very compact shape! **POINTS VALUE:** 50

DATE SPOTTED: **SPOT IT!**   **GOT IT!**

WHERE SPOTTED:

33

TERRIERS

NAME: Yorkshire Terrier **CLASS:** Terrier

You'll probably know me as a 'yorkie', one of the most popular doggie pet breeds. I was bred to catch and kill rats so I don't let my cute looks get in the way of my lively, alert nature! I have a compact, almost square-looking body due to my long coat which hangs almost dead straight nearly to the floor. **POINTS VALUE:** 10

DATE SPOTTED: **SPOT IT!** **GOT IT!**

WHERE SPOTTED:

NAME: Airedale Terrier **CLASS:** Terrier

I'm the largest of all the terriers, and my proud 'on tiptoe' bearing makes me appear even taller. As my name suggests, I was originally bred in Yorkshire, to hunt otters. More and more people are choosing me to be their household pet these days, and rightly so as I'm clever, devoted and protective! Watch out for my distinctive crinkly coat.

POINTS VALUE: 30

DATE SPOTTED: **SPOT IT!** **GOT IT!**

WHERE SPOTTED:

NAME: Bedlington Terrier | **CLASS:** Terrier

Despite my exotic looks, I was bred in Northumberland to catch rabbits. I may even be related to the whippet – just look at my racy shape! My pear-shaped head and nearly white 'top knot' also make me look very different to other breeds of terrier. At a gallop, I'm very fast. I can defend myself well when provoked and must be treated sensitively if I'm to be a loving companion. **POINTS VALUE:** 30

DATE SPOTTED: | SPOT IT! | GOT IT!
WHERE SPOTTED:

. . . .

NAME: Bull Terrier | **CLASS:** Terrier

I usually have a white coat and my Roman nose makes me easily recognisable. I'm brave and fiery, probably because I was bred from fighting dogs. However, don't be put off, I love humans and although can be a little obstinate, I'm fun and friendly. I was originally bred in Birmingham, England. **POINTS VALUE:** 20

DATE SPOTTED: | SPOT IT! | GOT IT!
WHERE SPOTTED:

NAME: Cairn Terrier **CLASS:** Terrier

Despite my size, I was
bred to hunt otters,
foxes and badgers
so I'm tough and
determined! My
weather-resistant
coat is particularly
helpful when it
comes to going
out in the most
extreme British
weather. We often have
dark-coloured points on our noses and tails.

POINTS VALUE: 20

DATE SPOTTED: **SPOT IT!** ✔ **GOT IT!**
WHERE SPOTTED:

· ·

NAME: Smooth Fox Terrier **CLASS:** Terrier

I'm not scared
of much,
which
means that
I'm suited to
'flushing' foxes
from their lairs
underground.
This also requires
me to have good
speed and stamina.
I'm an attractive dog
with my smooth coat and
intelligent expression, and with good handling,
make a faithful and lively house dog. I can also
catch rats! **POINTS VALUE:** 30

DATE SPOTTED: **SPOT IT!** **GOT IT!**
WHERE SPOTTED:

NAME: Irish Terrier   **CLASS:** Terrier

I'm foolhardy if I get into a scrap with another dog, but I make a great household pet as I love humans, especially children! When I'm 'set on' (about to go into hunting mode), I hold my head high.

POINTS VALUE: 40

DATE SPOTTED: 16.7.06   **SPOT IT!** ✓   **GOT IT!**

WHERE SPOTTED: Pornock caravan park

• •

NAME: Jack Russell   **CLASS:** Terrier

I owe my name to a keen huntsman, Parson Jack Russell, who started the breed in the nineteenth century. However, we were not recognised officially by the Kennel Club until 1990. **POINTS VALUE:** 10

DATE SPOTTED: 14\3\07   **SPOT IT!** ✓   **GOT IT!**

WHERE SPOTTED: on The road

• •

NAME: Kerry Blue   **CLASS:** Terrier

Perhaps my most distinctive feature is my gorgeous, blue-grey, soft, silky coat which actually looks as if it has been 'knitted'. As terriers go, I'm one of the larger breeds, bred in Ireland and I carry all the terrier characteristics of bravery, faithfulness and determination. **POINTS VALUE:** 50

DATE SPOTTED: **SPOT IT!**   **GOT IT!**

WHERE SPOTTED:

43

NAME: Manchester Terrier　**CLASS:** Terrier

I look pretty different to most of the terriers you'll find on this page as I've got a very smooth, glossy coat which is often black and tan in colouring. Whilst I look elegant, and make a good house dog, keep an eye out for my slightly wilful nature – I was bred to catch rats, and I certainly haven't lost the knack!

POINTS VALUE: 20

DATE SPOTTED:　**SPOT IT!**　**GOT IT!**

WHERE SPOTTED:

NAME: Skye Terrier　**CLASS:** Terrier

I may look slightly comical as I'm almost twice as long as I am high! Despite being low to the ground, however, I'm very solidly built. My lovely long coat does need a lot of grooming but I'll reward my owner for their time as I'm a real one-person dog. My undying loyalty makes me wary of strangers, so I'm an impressive guard.

POINTS VALUE: 30

DATE SPOTTED:　**SPOT IT!**　**GOT IT!**

WHERE SPOTTED:

(**NAME:** Soft-Coated Wheaten Terrier)

(**CLASS:** Terrier)

Pure bred 'wheaties' really do have a coat the colour of corn. I'm an Irish breed, like the Kerry Blue, and a tough, hardy type. My sporting instinct is still quite strong and I've bags of energy. A

good job, really, as I was bred to round up cattle. Even though my coat looks like it needs a good brush, it actually looks after itself rather well. **POINTS VALUE:** 40

(**DATE SPOTTED:**) (**SPOT IT!** (**GOT IT!**

(**WHERE SPOTTED:**)

• •

(**NAME:** Pit Bull Terrier) (**CLASS:** Terrier)

I am very much like the Staffordshire Bull except that my ears do not flop forward as theirs do. I'm quite muscly and need plenty of exercise to make sure I don't become overweight. Pit bulls were originally bred for dogfighting, therefore, I can be rather aggressive unless very well trained. **POINTS VALUE:** 20

(**DATE SPOTTED:**) (**SPOT IT!** (**GOT IT!**

(**WHERE SPOTTED:**)

45

NAME: Welsh Terrier | **CLASS:** Terrier

Although I'm not shy, I'm definitely one of the quieter members of the terrier family. This makes me a good pet, especially around less boisterous or nervous children. I'm also easily controlled. I was originally bred in Wales to hunt foxes. **POINTS VALUE:** 30

| DATE SPOTTED: | SPOT IT! | GOT IT! |

| WHERE SPOTTED: |

NAME: West Highland White Terrier
CLASS: Terrier

I'm an alert little dog and great as a household pet due to my small size and love of children. You've got to like getting up and doing things though, because I always want to be at the centre of the action and like to devise new games to play! The only thing I ask is that owners keep my wavy coat nicely clipped.

POINTS VALUE: 10

| DATE SPOTTED: | SPOT IT! ✓ | GOT IT! |

| WHERE SPOTTED: |

NAME: Wire Fox Terrier

CLASS: Terrier

I look quite different to my cousin, the Smooth Fox Terrier, with a dense, rough coat that makes me look bigger than I really am. With my earnest expression and happy personality, I'm ready for anything.

POINTS VALUE: 20

DATE SPOTTED:	SPOT IT!	GOT IT!
WHERE SPOTTED:		

. . . .

NAME: Glen of Imaal Terrier   **CLASS:** Terrier

I take my name from a glen in County Wicklow, Ireland, where I was first bred. I'm a fairly small terrier, quiet around the home and silent whilst working. I make a devoted family pet.

POINTS VALUE: 50

DATE SPOTTED:	SPOT IT!	GOT IT!
WHERE SPOTTED:		

. . . .

NAME: Sealyham Terrier   **CLASS:** Terrier

I take my name from Sealyham House near Haverfordwest in Wales. My very square jaw and almost oblong shape gives an impression of hardiness, and I'm very much the brisk, workmanlike dog who also lives happily alongside the family. **POINTS VALUE:** 20

DATE SPOTTED:	SPOT IT!	GOT IT!
WHERE SPOTTED:		

Index

Photographs supplied by Sally Anne Thompson and R. T. Willbie/Animal Photography and Corel.